It's Your Time Now:
What Will You Do With It?

It's Your Time Now: What Will You Do With It?

◆

An 8-Week Plan for Figuring Out the What's Next in Your Life

Mary Guarino, Ph.D.

iUniverse, Inc.

New York Lincoln Shanghai

It's Your Time Now: What Will You Do With It?
An 8-Week Plan for Figuring Out the What's Next in Your Life

iUniverse, Inc.

For information address:
iUniverse, Inc.
2021 Pine Lake Road, Suite 100
Lincoln, NE 68512
www.iuniverse.com

ISBN: 0-595-30320-X

Printed in the United States of America

This Book is Dedicated to

Julia and Kia, my much-wiser-than-me daughters and unending sources of inspiration

Contents

Introduction xi

How to Use This Workbook xvii

First Things First: Making Time xix

CHAPTER 1   Getting to the Core 1

CHAPTER 2   What Do You Want in a Job? 4

CHAPTER 3   Open Your Eyes to Possibility 9

CHAPTER 4   Pay Attention to Your Dreams 13

CHAPTER 5   What's Your Style? 17

CHAPTER 6   Take Inventory of Your Transferable Skills 22

CHAPTER 7   You Gotta Have Friends 26

CHAPTER 8   So What's Next? 30

Values Log 33

Dream Diary 35

Good Stuff Log 37

Ideal Work Environment Log 39

Achievement Inventory 41

About the Author 43

Acknowledgements

I want to thank the participants in my workshops, from whom I've gained much insight, and with whom I've greatly enjoyed working. Thank you, also, to Gail Minthorn, my long-time friend, for her valuable feedback on the manuscript for *It's Your Time Now*, as well as Morgan O'Brien for his expert views in the area of human resources. I also want to thank all the researchers who have come before me who have done much to understand the psychology of work, and what makes us happy.

Mary Guarino, Ph.D.
Weston, CT
December 2003

Introduction

"They say that time changes things, but you actually have to change them yourself."

—*Andy Warhol*

After her daughter was born 10 years ago, Angela had taken a part-time position with her husband's company. When her daughter was a baby, the job gave her the ability to work from home, and over time it remained flexible, allowing her time to drive her daughter to school, and accompany her to play dates and after school activities. While her contribution to the company was important in many ways, she never felt fulfilled by it. She stayed with it because it worked for her family. During the two years before she took my workshop, the post-Internet-boom economic downturn had caused her husband's company to fall into hard times, so now she not only had the goal of finding a more meaningful job, but one that would pay well and allow her to bring in needed additional income for her family.

During the course of the workshop, Angela took inventory of her skills, interests and core values. And, through a series of self-assessments, group exercises and discussion, she began to get in touch with the aspects of herself that she had put aside long ago. She recalled, for the first time in many years, that she had wanted to be a dancer when she was a young woman, but was discouraged by her father who instead urged her on the path into the corporate world. So, for several years before her daughter was born, Angela had held various high-powered positions in male-dominated business settings. While very successful, she admitted that she never felt very happy in these types of environments: "It was as if I had to put on a mask to walk into work each day, a mask that I would take off as soon as I left the office."

As we worked on identifying her core values, skills and interests, Angela began to see that the times in her life when she felt in balance included two years spent overseas in a job where she fully utilized her excellent business and fluent Spanish language skills. She recalled that she had also felt very happy when she was involved, for several years, in a volunteer position for a nonprofit community organization.

Soon after making these revelations, Angela began to express a desire to do something with her life that would utilize her Spanish language, fundraising and nonprofit development skills, and would make a difference for others. She is now in a position with a nonprofit organization that connects Hispanic families with various public services available to them. Her duties include development work as well as direct contact with the families. It also provides flexibility in scheduling so that she can be there to pick up her daughter from school each day. And it pays very well, allowing her to bring a much-needed second income to her family. It also fully affirmed that Angela could stay true to her core values including family, helping others, cultural diversity and growth, while working in a job that she enjoys. She reframed the "reality" that had been created throughout her life regarding the concept of what work should be, and finally pursued a career path that best honored her true self.

It's Your Time Now: What Will You Do With It? is based on the workshop in which Angela was a participant. I created the workshop specifically for women who are considering changing careers or re-entering the workforce after many years of being full-time mothers. The workshop participants have the common experience of focusing on their families and not on themselves, and most have spent so many years thinking of what is best for others that they have fallen out of touch with what makes them happiest.

In considering this big transition, many of my workshop participants have experienced feelings of guilt and anxiety over the idea of going back to work, choosing a path that will be fulfilling to them, or even just focusing on their own needs for a while. But I assure them that research has shown that work and family can definitely mix, and can be very beneficial for women and their families. Nancy Marshall, a researcher at Wellesley College, found that women who work and have children, while experiencing more stress than women without children, benefit from having dual roles. It seems that having two major focuses in their lives helps to mitigate stresses that may occur in one area or the other. In other words, when things are stressful at work, working mothers gain comfort and strength from their home lives, and vice versa. These benefits have been found to hold true to for men with families, too.

In addition, working does not appear to have detrimental effects on children's development. Psychologist Elizabeth Harvey analyzed data that had been collected over a period of 20 years for the National Longitudinal Survey of Youth. She found that children whose mothers worked during their first five years of life were not significantly different in terms of obedience, behavioral problems, cognitive development, self-esteem or academic achievement.

I begin each workshop by telling my story of career change and self-discovery. I've been there, and although each of us will have unique situations, challenges and aspirations, there are many common threads for all of us who are trying to figure out what we want to be when we grow up...

At age 26, I had my first mid-life crisis. My younger daughter would soon be heading off to full-day kindergarten, and my career as a self-employed graphic designer, while flexible and perfect while I was full-time parenting, was also quite unfulfilling. I found myself thinking, "I'm going to have a lot more time on my hands once both of my children are in school all day. And before I know it, they will be off to college! Once my career doesn't need to adapt to my children's schedules, what should I being doing with my time? This is not what I want to be doing for the rest of my life."

While I enjoyed the creative aspects of graphic design, I began to yearn for something that would be intellectually stimulating in a different way. Furthermore, I wanted to do something that would actually help people. I began to seek out books and self-administered tests related to career exploration. As I waded through tons of resources, and spoke to various people, I found that the idea of "psychology" as a career path kept coming up for me. I found this perplexing as I had never taken a psychology course, and had a perception of psychology as Freudian psychoanalysis, which I did not feel was a good fit with my view of people and life. Also, I had always considered myself an artist—I had been told from a very young age that I was gifted in that area, and that was the identity that others had reinforced in me. However, the idea of psychology continued to present itself to me, so I began to look into it.

I was surprised to find that there were many perspectives in psychology, and that one didn't have to adhere to any single one to be a psychologist. I began to realize that psychology can be used to help people in many different ways, not just through analysis and other clinical techniques. And I discovered the area of lifespan developmental psychology, which focuses on understanding and supporting the healthy growth and functioning of individuals from birth through death.

So, I began to take psychology courses, and found that I really enjoyed them. The more I learned about the vast and varied field of psychology, the more I grew to love it. And, about three-and-a-half years after beginning my quest to figure out what to do with the rest of my life, I was accepted into a doctoral program in

Lifespan Developmental Psychology. Thus began my journey of self-discovery, which still continues.

I always ask the participants what brought them to the workshop. Many have been focusing on family, either staying at home full-time or working in a capacity that fits the family, but is certainly not their calling. Some, like Angela, have to step up their earning capacity because of a downsized spouse. Some are just ready for the next challenge, but don't know what that might be. The one thing they all have in common is their readiness to make a change, or at least begin the journey of discovering the best career for them, and an unwillingness to just go with what is familiar or easy. Rather, they want to discover the career and/or educational path that will be most fulfilling and challenging for them, and is also in alignment with their core values.

What has brought you to this book?

No matter what your reason for starting this journey, kudos goes out to you for taking the initiative. You have taken the first step toward uncovering the multitude of possibilities that are out there waiting for you. *It's Your Time Now* takes a holistic approach to career change—it asks you look within yourself for strengths, to take inventory of your existing personal resources, then asks you to step out beyond this to discover your next steps.

My workshop participants have told me that these exercises have helped them to see things in a new way, to become aware of things about themselves that had been not-so-obvious to them, and to focus and move forward steadily toward their goals. Many have been surprised by their discoveries and have attained a new energy around creating a path towards what they want. One workshop participant was surprised to remember how passionate she had been about becoming a missionary in her early life! As a full-time mother for the past 20 years, this was a dream that she had never realized. Even though it was not a career she felt she could undertake fully during this phase of her life, she did start to make plans to participate in shorter-term projects, such as trips to South America to help build schools with church groups. In this way, she was addressing her passion, not saying, "I'd love to do that, but it's impossible," and taking an attainable first step that will enable her to see if this type of work will truly make her happy.

I believe that the beauty in career change lies in the journey. There is not necessarily one correct path for you—there could be several viable paths you can take. The purpose of *It's Your Time Now* is to expand your mind, and open your eyes to the possibilities by making you aware of your core interests and values, as well as alerting you to the myriad resources and opportunities all around you.

The "what's next" that you create from these exercises should be part of the wonder filled journey that is your life.

How to Use This Workbook

"Change has a considerable psychological impact on the human mind. To the fearful it is threatening because it means that things may get worse. To the hopeful it is encouraging because things may get better. To the confident it is inspiring because the challenge exists to make things better."

—*King Whitney, Jr.*

"It's not that some people have willpower and some don't. It's that some people are ready to change and others are not."

—*James Gordon, M.D.*

Each chapter in *It's Your Time Now* contains exercises designed to help you figure out what career or educational path might be most interesting for you. This is achieved through a step-by-step process of first looking within yourself, then reaching out beyond your every day habits to fully assess your possibilities.

Although you are certainly welcome to complete this book at any pace that works for you, the exercises are most beneficial if you take a few days to work on each set of exercises. Ideally, you should set aside about 15 to 30 minutes per day to work on this, with the goal of completing one chapter each week. This will allow you adequate time to ponder, assimilate, and reflect on your self-discoveries. And this is quite achievable, even with the constraints of a busy schedule.

Most of the chapters in *It's Your Time Now* contain self-assessment exercises for you to work through. At the end of each chapter, you will find a thought-provoking query (labeled "Food for Thought"), which you should ponder during the time between chapters. As thoughts come to you related to each query, write them down in the space provided at the end of the chapter. Each chapter also concludes with "Your Assignment," which is the task, or tasks, you are to work on during the week between chapters. At the end of each chapter, there is a list of selected resources in case you would like to delve further into the chapter's topic.

By setting aside just 30 minutes or less per day to work on the assignments in this book, you will begin to gain insight into yourself, and develop a clearer idea of the types of work that will be most fulfilling for you. This will create a solid foundation upon which to begin your career path journey.

It's Your Time Now contains the following chapters, which will take you step-by-step through the process of identifying possible educational and career directions that should be most interesting for you to pursue:

- Chapter 1: Getting to the Core
- Chapter 2: What Do You Want in a Job?
- Chapter 3: Open Your Eyes to Possibility
- Chapter 4: Pay Attention to Your Dreams
- Chapter 5: What's Your Style?
- Chapter 6: You Gotta Have Friends
- Chapter 7: Take Inventory of Your Transferable Skills
- Chapter 8: So, What's Next?

There are also supplemental sections, including diaries and logs. You may want to make copies of these pages, or you may even want to start separate journals for each of these sections so that you will have plenty of space to record your thoughts and discoveries:

- First Things First: Making Time
- Values Log
- Dream Diary
- Good Stuff Log
- Ideal Work Environment Log
- Achievement Inventory

So, when will you set aside time each week to work on this?

Days_____ Times _____

First Things First: Making Time

"Until you value yourself, you won't value your time. Until you value your time, you will not do anything with it."

—M Scott Peck

If you are a mom, it probably comes as no surprise to you that, while 80% of American women recognize they should take time for themselves, almost none of them actually do. A recent study conducted by The Thymes Limited (an aromatherapy bath product company) in conjunction with IPSOS-ASI (an international research firm) found that most American women with children spend several hours per day caring for their families. However, 92% of those with one child, and 96% of those with more than one child, say they don't even spend one hour per day doing something just for themselves. This is despite the fact that the vast majority know that self-nurturing is important to the well-being of themselves and, by osmosis, their families.

At first, many of my workshop participants express feelings of guilt about taking time away from their families to do something as "self-indulgent" as pondering what they want to do next in their lives. Over time, though, they come to the realization that it is not only to their benefit, but to the benefit of their families for them to live as whole, self-actualized individuals. It's a win-win situation!

Completing this workbook will take a consistent, concerted effort on your part, and will require that you set time aside to work on the various exercises. Making the most of your precious time in an important part of your self-development efforts. Following are some tips for optimizing your available time. These techniques help me to balance my time now, and also helped me get through the process of raising children while working full-time and writing my dissertation. These tips apply to life in general, and can also be very helpful if you are in the process of a career change while living an already busy life.

- Set aside a certain amount of time each day just to do what you want to do (like work on the tasks in this book!)—how about 1 hour each day?

- If that's not "possible," start with smaller increments of time (say 15 minutes) and adjust the amount of time upward, as you are able to do so.

xx   It's Your Time Now: What Will You Do With It?

Doing part of something is better than doing nothing—even if you can't complete a task or a project, it is better to take a small "chunk" out of it rather than letting the whole thing sit until later

- Learn to say "No"—this is not always easy, but it can make a world of difference. Even if you don't want to say "No" completely, try to set limits around how much you will do and when (it should fit within your schedule)

- Bundle your tasks—save up non-urgent errands so that you can do those that are logistically close to one another

- Delegate—how much is your time worth? It may be worth the cost of hiring someone to do things like mow your lawn, clean your house, AND you will be purchasing the precious commodity of Time. It's more than okay to ask for help

- If you must do something (like fill out forms), and it will take less than 5 minutes, do it immediately. The little things add up.

- Do the yucky stuff first—take care of the tasks that you dislike so that you don't waste precious mental time ruminating about not having done them!

- Are the things you feel you "have" to do really necessary? It can be easy to get caught up in the details to the detriment of the big picture.

- And, set aside time each week for something special—make sure that, no matter how busy you are, you take time to play. Spending time with friends, outdoors, at the movies, whatever makes you happy, is essential in helping you be the most focused and effective you can be with your time

- Take a look at the activities and people in your life that are "energy drainers"—do they need to be part of your life? What would happen if you eliminated or reduced your time spent on/with them?

- Take time for mental and physical exercise—just half an hour of yoga, walking, running, meditating or journaling can give you enhanced energy and mental clarity, making the time you do have much more efficient

It's your time now. Make the most of it!

1

Getting to the Core

"Happiness is that state of consciousness which proceeds from the achievement of one's values."

—*Ayn Rand*

"He who knows others is wise. He who knows himself is enlightened."

—*Lao Tzu*

As you begin your journey of discovering the most satisfying next chapter in your life, it is helpful to gain a clear picture of your core values. Core values are the intangible things that are deeply and uniquely important to each of us. We all have our own particular set of values, which, when we honor them in our day-to-day lives, make us feel happy and in balance. Our values might include things like "integrity," "joy," "physical fitness," "family," "spirituality," "community," "challenge," or "creativity." While things such as wealth, travel and fashion can represent or provide manifestations of our values, they are not values themselves. Rather, values are who we are. They represent our unique selves, and our most fulfilling manner of relating to people and situations.

Core values are the things that really make life meaningful, interesting, and fulfilling for each of us. And, therefore, understanding our core values is a very important step in determining how we should live our individual lives. By examining the extent to which we honor our values in our day-to-day lives, we can gain great insight into areas of our lives that need to be brought into balance, and find it easier to make informed choices regarding what we should be doing. When we live in a manner that is out of sync with our values, we live a life that is less than fulfilling, often one that we "deal with" rather than enjoy. Such a life often feels lacking in joy.

Angela, whose story was told in the Introduction, is a classic example of someone who redesigned her life in a way that brought it in line with her core values.

1

When she worked in an environment that was not a good fit with her values, she felt as if she were playing a role, wearing a mask, one that she was all too happy to shed when she left the office. And now, she is living in a way in which her work and personal life are both in balance, and is truly honoring her core values.

When we live in a manner that is in alignment with our core values, we are happy, effective and more pleasant to be around. Psychologist Mihaly Csikszentmihalyi of the University of Chicago has been studying the idea of "happiness" for over 30 years. His research has consistently shown that, when people are engaged in an activity that is challenging and meaningful to them, they feel in control of their actions, and time passes easily and they express feelings of great satisfaction. Csikszentmihalyi calls this "optimal experience" or "flow." The most important thing to understand about flow is that we are each responsible for making it happen for ourselves. Csikszentmihalyi has found that "people who learn to control inner experience are able to determine the quality of their lives."

Lisa, one of my life coaching clients, had "fallen" into marketing research 8 years before I met her. She was very good at her job and had the respect of everyone with whom she had worked. Yet marketing research didn't provide meaning for her and didn't enhance her life in any way. In working with her, Lisa came up with a list of her core values, which included "helping people," "continually discovering new ideas" and "making a difference." Her desire to find a different line of work stemmed from the fact that she wanted to do something more rewarding with her life. After a while, she realized that she had always had an interest in epidemiology (the study of diseases) but had never done anything to pursue it.

After working through a series of exercises in self-assessment, job research and coaching, Lisa decided to make the leap from her known world of marketing research, and is now pursuing a master's degree in genetic epidemiology.

One of the most effective ways in which to uncover and discover our core values is to think about our lives, and the times in which we felt very happy or "in the zone." Conversely, when we think about the occasions in which we felt extremely unhappy, angry, frustrated or upset, we can identify times when we were living in a way that was in opposition to our values. Identifying these very positive and very negative situations can provide us with important clues as to the things in our lives that were in or out of sync with our core values. Thinking about such times can reveal ways in which you can make future decisions that honor your values, and avoid situations that will be out of alignment with your deep-seated needs.

As you work on the exercises in this chapter, it is important to think about your core values in terms of who you are, not who you would *like* to be, or feel that you *should* be. Remember that your core values reflect the true you, the you that is a wonderful unique individual in the world. When you have a clear, thorough understanding of your core values, you hold in your hands a powerful tool for pointing yourself in the direction of a career path, and a life, that is most fulfilling.

So, what are your values?

Food for Thought:

Are you living your life in a manner that reflects your values?
Do you spend your time in a way that is consistent with your priorities?

Your Assignment:

1. Ask yourself, "What things are important to me?" Write down everything that comes to mind in the Values Log at the back of this book. Keep adding to this list over the next week.

2. Next, think of a time when you were extremely motivated. What were you thinking and feeling right before then? Again, repeat this exercise during the course of the next week. This will provide you with another list of values to add to your Values Log.

3. Examine the entries in your Values Log. Are there any pairs of values that in are conflict with one another for you? For example, do you want "Independence" and "Community" or "Wealth" and "Spirituality"? For each of these pairs, think about ways in which you may be able to honor both without compromising one or the other.

Recommended Reading

How to Practice: The Way to a Meaningful Life

His Holiness the Dalai Lama and Jeffrey Hopkins (Pocket Star, 1991).

Flow: The Psychology of Optimal Experience

Mihaly Csikszentmihalyi (Harper & Row, 1990)

2

What Do You Want in a Job?

"Never continue in a job you don't enjoy. If you're happy in what you're doing, you'll like yourself; you'll have inner peace. And if you have that, along with physical health, you will have had more success than you could possibly have imagined."

—*Johnny Carson*

"Pleasure in the job puts perfection in the work."

—*Aristotle*

"Whoever does not love his work cannot hope that it will please others."

—*Unknown*

Now that you have had time to ponder your core values, it is time to think about those things that are important to you in your work environment. As I have already mentioned, in order for your work to be satisfying, it should be in alignment with your core values. You will also have work-specific values, as well as job characteristics, which will be important in choosing a environment that feels comfortable and satisfying to you.

When you acknowledge and live in alignment with your core values in the work that you do, you will naturally bring energy and enthusiasm to your work. This is very important in the ever-changing world of the new economy. As things change around you, if you are doing what feels right to you, you are more likely to be your best, and to be happiest. When you have a good fit between your core values and your work, it feels relatively easy. It shouldn't be a strain to fit into your work environment—if it is very uncomfortable, something isn't right. A few of my workshop participants, like Angela, have endured careers where they put on an entirely different persona for work, which they gladly removed when they went home each day. Angela created a complete separation of work and life,

4

never engaging in social activities with her colleagues. As I've mentioned, she was extremely successful in her career in terms of promotions and very high salaries, but this double life caused large amounts of stress for her in both her careers and personal life.

If you are an adult, you have had plenty of time to explore various career ideas, and to develop opinions as to which careers are suitable or not for you. But, you also have a lifetime of self-judgment, and having people who are close to you, many well-intentioned, promoting their ideas as to what you are or are not good at, and what you "should" be doing. A friend who has a successful PR practice told me that when she announced to her family that she planned to leave her established corporate career and start her own business, her mother said, "But you're not good at that, dear." For the longest time, another friend, who is earning his doctorate in biostatistics, was told by his teachers and parents that he was not good at math. In order to get into graduate school, he had to take the GREs and was surprised to obtain a 790 in the math section!

As you go through the following exercises, ignore the voices in your head! Think about those activities and job categories that are of interest to you, regardless of whether or not you currently have the skills, or even have experience in those areas. Just go with the things that spark your interest.

These exercises will help you gain a general idea of where your work interests lie. If you are interested in taking a formal validated career interest assessment, "Self-Directed Search," is available through Psychological Assessment Resources, Inc. (PAR) as an online version that takes about 15 minutes and costs less than $10. I have provided the website address for PAR at the end of this chapter.

Gallup, the public opinion polling organization, recently surveyed 300,000 companies and found that between 50 and 60 percent of employees are not doing their best work, and another 15 to 20 percent are "actively disengaged" (not caring about their work, and often not even showing up!), because they are not in the least excited about their work, and do not see the meaning in it. This costs companies billions of dollars per year—Gallup estimates that if 100 percent of employees were fully engaged in their work, customers would be 70 percent more loyal, turnover would decrease by 70 percent, and profits would increase by 40 percent.

It seems obvious that you should be in a job that makes you happy, and that companies should do their best to make their employees happy, but, unfortunately, this is not always the case. However, since you are in the process of creating a custom-fitted career path, you have the ability, you could even say the *responsibility*, to make sure that you choose an environment that is a good fit with who you are and what you need.

Food for Thought:

Which aspects of your past jobs have you loved?
Which aspects have you despised?
If you could do *anything* you wanted to do for your career, and money was not a factor, what would you do?

Your Assignment:

Answer the following questions:

1. What work schedule best suits you?
2. What work environment helps you to be most productive?
3. What is the best way for you to approach a big project?
4. What time of day are you most productive?
5. What time of day are you least productive?
6. How do you handle stress on the job?
7. How do you maintain balance between work and the rest of your life?

Now look at the following job characteristics and think about which ones resonate with you. Write down the characteristics that appeal to you in the Ideal Work Environment Log at the back of this book. Add any other characteristics that are important to you, but are not included in the list. Over the next several days, review the list and add to it as you think of new items.

- Autonomy
- Arranging your own hours, working according to your time schedule
- Variety
- Working outdoors
- Performing regular, predictable tasks

- Physical challenge

- Intellectual challenge

- Working in an environment fueled by deadlines

- Performing exacting tasks that leave little room for error

- Having the power to make choices about what to do and how to do it

- Pursuing knowledge and understanding; continual learning

- Creativity

- Developing new and different ideas, products, programs or systems

- Contributing to society

- Gaining public recognition for your contributions

- Working to uphold a set of moral and ethical standards

- Spiritual growth

- Having contact with a variety of people

- Teaching others

- Working alone

- Working with individuals from a variety of backgrounds

- Working in teams

- Helping others

- Influencing others

- Being in a position to oversee the work of other employees

Recommended Reading

The Art of Happiness at Work

> His Holiness the Dalai Lama and Howard C. Cutler (Riverhead Books, 2003)

Let Your Life Speak: Listening for the Voice of Vocation

> Parker J. Palmer. (Jossey-Bass, 1999).

Making Vocational Choices: A Theory of Careers

> John L. Holland, Ph.D. (Prentice Hall, 1973)

Web Resources

Self-Directed Search—based on the work of psychologist John Holland, this 15-minute online survey can help you to determine which types of work environments would be most compatible with your interests.
http://www.self-directed-search.com/

3

Open Your Eyes to Possibility

"A discovery is said to be an accident meeting a prepared mind."
　　　　　　　　　　　　　　　　　　　—Albert von Szent-Gyorgyi

"Chance is always powerful. Let your hook be always cast; in the pool where you least expect it, there will be a fish."

　　　　　　　　　　　　　　　　　　　　　　　　　—Ovid

"I'm a great believer in luck, and I find the harder I work the more I have of it."

　　　　　　　　　　　　　　　　　　　　　—Thomas Jefferson

For the past 40 years, psychologists have studied the factors that make people more or less successful in the things that they do. Three major theories that have emerged during that time include Julius Rotter's Locus of Control, Martin Seligman's Learned Optimism and Albert Bandura's Self-efficacy.

The idea behind Rotter's Locus of Control is that people differ in the amount of control they feel they have over events in their lives. People with a high sense of Internal Locus of Control attribute their successes and failures to their own abilities and actions, and believe that every individual is responsible for the outcomes of his or her activities. People who have high Internal Locus of Control tend to take command of situations and overcome obstacles. Locus of Control is the basis for Learned Optimism, Self-efficacy and the new Luck Theory.

Seligman's Learned Optimism is based on the premise that we can choose how we view the things that happen to us, and the more positive we are, the better we will fare. Not only are people who take an optimistic view of the events in their lives happier, they are also healthier, and recover from physical and emotional setbacks much faster than people with pessimistic viewpoints. For Optimists, problems are seen as temporary, specific and external, rather than a reflection of

9

their failure as a person. If individuals can learn to tell themselves Optimistic things like, 'Things didn't go well today, but I learned a lot from the experience, and I'll do better tomorrow," they have a much better chance of overcoming adversity. There are many physical as well as psychological benefits to an Optimistic outlook: Seligman found that students who participated in a workshop he created to cultivate Learned Optimism had much lower rates of depression, anxiety and illness than a comparable group that did not participate in the workshop. Research and programs that have been created based on Learned Optimism provide a scientific foundation for many of the claims made by the self-help field.

Albert Bandura's Self-efficacy concept has to do with your belief in your own ability to do things, which in turn affects the way you behave in various situations. People who have high Self-efficacy are confident in themselves, will try more things and display a more positive attitude toward everything they encounter. People with high Self-efficacy see tasks as challenges, apply a lot of effort to the tasks they undertake, stick to these tasks, overcome adversity, and seek out solutions to the problems they encounter. They believe they have the ability to change their environment to effect a change they desire. Simply believing in yourself can greatly enhance your chances of achieving positive change.

Together, this research shows that the best results happen for people who take control of their own situations, learn from negative experiences and see life's tasks as interesting challenges.

Most recently, at the University of Hertfordshire in England, psychologist Richard Wiseman has been studying "lucky" versus "unlucky" people. He has found that good things tend to happen to people who see the positive in all situations. It appears to be true that seeing opportunity, even in disaster, can open up possibilities for many things in your life. By focusing on the things that you want, you set the stage for seeing opportunities as they come along.

In his research, Wiseman found that people who reported consistent "good fortune" throughout their lives tend to be open to new ideas and experiences, and are prepared to take risks on new opportunities. "Unlucky" people, on the other hand, tend to get stuck in a rut—they shy away from new experiences and ideas.

Bandura also believed that chance encounters, combined with an open positive attitude, can result in great opportunities that can change one's life for the better. In his 1982 article "The Psychology of Chance Encounters and Life Paths," Bandura discussed how personal initiative creates opportunities where they are more likely to encounter life-changing "lucky" events. Even though there is much in life that is out of our control, Bandura believed that we can make chance work for us through self-development, and an openness to opportunities.

While we cannot control all of the things that life will throw our way, the work of psychologists such as Wiseman, Rotter, Seligman and Bandura shows us that we can certainly control how we see these events and how we react to them, all to our benefit.

Here are Wiseman's four keys to "Good Luck", which you can integrate into your daily life:

1. Create, notice and act upon chance opportunities. Take advantage of chance opportunities by being open to new ideas and experiences, adopting a flexible and relaxed attitude toward life, and building and maintaining a strong network of individuals in your life (this book devotes an entire chapter, "You Gotta Have Friends," to the importance of social support networks).

2. Cultivate your intuition, then listen to it! Listen to your gut feelings and hunches about people and situations. Those dreams and gut feelings are telling you something important. Develop and nurture your intuitive abilities through meditation, prayer and taking a few minutes each day to clear your mind. You can also hone your intuitive skills by keeping a dream journal (see the chapter "Pay Attention to Your Dreams" in this book for tips on harnessing the important messages that can be found in your dreams).

3. Always look at the bright side of life: See the glass as half full. By taking a positive perspective on life, you will see the opportunities, even within the disappointments. Expectations usually become self-fulfilling prophecy. When you expect things to turn out for the best, you are more likely to persist in the face of failure and positively shape your interactions with others.

4. Turn bad luck into good luck: When life gives you lemons, well, you know what to do...Try to see how things might have been worse. Don't ruminate about how bad things are. Rather, take control of the situation and think of ways in which you might be able to use it to your advantage.

Food for Thought:

Do you generally see the glass as half full or half empty?

Your Assignment:

At the end of each day for the next week, write down all the good things that have happened to you, and ONLY the good things, in your Good Stuff Log. At the end of the week, take a look at all the good stuff you've encountered. Keep this list going for as long as you can and observe what a charmed life you are living!

Recommended Reading

The Luck Factor: Changing Your Luck, Changing Your Life: Four Essential Factors
   Richard Wiseman, Ph.D. (Miramax, 2003).

Learned Optimism: How to Change Your Mind and Your Life
   Martin Seligman, Ph.D. (Pocket Books, 1998).

Web Resources

The Luck Factor—Dr. Richard Wiseman's website
   http://www.luckfactor.co.uk

4

Pay Attention to Your Dreams

"To accomplish great things, we must dream as well as act."

—*Anatole France*

"All men who have achieved great things have been great dreamers."

—*Orison Swett Marden*

In our information-filled, fast-paced, high stress, modern lives, we often miss the signals coming from our "gut," our intuition, our subconscious. We concentrate on the task at hand, and rely on the physical and the logical. However, as I discussed in the last chapter, "Open Your Eyes to the Possibilities," it is important to listen to your inner voice if you want to maximize your chances for positive opportunities. Dreams, which communicate with us through metaphor and symbols, can provide us with some of the valuable intuitive information that we may be missing during our waking hours. Dreams offer us insight into the issues we face, with the advantage of a very different perspective than we would normally take. Dreams can provide us with insight into areas of our lives that need attention and can point us toward the things we should be noticing, the directions we should be taking. And they can be very useful in helping us uncover some of the key components necessary for finding satisfaction in our work-lives.

Many great scientific and creative insights were obtained through dreams. Here are just a few of the better known examples of creations and discoveries that came about as a result of people paying attention to the information in their dreams:

- The writing of Robert Louis Stevenson and Edgar Allen Poe is known to have been inspired by their dreams;

- The German chemist, Friedrich A. Kekulé, visualized the molecular structure of benzene (a closed carbon ring) after seeing it represented as a snake eating it's own tale in a dream;

13

- After dreaming of how horses run at the race track, Niels Bohr formulated his quantum theory, for which he was awarded a Nobel Prize;

- As a young man, Albert Einstein dreamed that he was sledding down a steep mountainside, faster and faster, approaching the speed of light, causing the stars to change their appearance. This became the inspiration for his theory of relativity;

- Carl Jung wrote of his early dream journals, "All my works, all my creative activity, has come from those initial fantasies and dreams which began in 1912, almost fifty years ago. Everything that I accomplished in later life was already contained in them, although at first only in the form of emotions and images."

Dream experts say that our dreams depict elements of our personalities—all of the people in our dreams represent different aspects of ourselves, which can provide valuable insight into our current situations and our selves. Jung believed that, "If we meditate on a dream sufficiently long and thoroughly, if we carry it around with us and turn it over and over, something almost always comes of it."

Although dreams are often difficult to understand because they present themselves in symbols and pictures, we can work toward understanding them by figuring out their relationships to our current situation. For example, Linda, one of my workshop participants, dreamed she was asked to drive one of two 18-wheelers containing rental supplies, including tables and chairs from her son's birthday party. The other truck was to be driven by her husband. She felt anxious and fearful at the prospect, thinking to herself, "I don't know how to drive one of these things!" But her husband assured her that she did have the knowledge and skill. Linda was contemplating returning to work after being a full-time mother for 18 years, and had concerns regarding several aspects of this transition. By examining her dreams, she confirmed that she felt she had the real-life support of her husband. As she talked about the dream she realized that one of her biggest fears was that she wouldn't be competent in a new work setting. We worked on addressing her fears by having her take inventory of her past achievements, interests and skills. And she came to realize that she had much going for her in terms of inner and outer resources.

As you begin to examine your dreams, you should contemplate each image or symbol until it begins to make sense to you. If there is someone you feel comfortable talking to about your dreams, they can be a good resource for helping you to gain insight into your dreams.

Dreams can symbolize several different things for you: at times they may represent things you have experienced during the day; other times the may represent things you experienced in the past; and at other times they are just plain weird! What is dreamed is not as important as why the dreamer had such a dream at this particular moment, and why he felt he had that particular experience. Even when we dream of things that actually happened, the story is often adapted to include details, people or circumstances that were not present in real life, but that should be taken into account when attempting to understand it.

You can gain a great deal more insight into the messages behind your dreams by taking into consideration several days' worth of dreams. A series of dreams, when evaluated in the context of one another, can highlight recurring themes, and can indicate important issues to which you should pay attention.

Jung felt that it is important for the dreamer to understand his own dreams. He encouraged individuals to record their dreams carefully, and even to illustrate them with pictures. This is definitely something everyone can do (no artistic ability is necessary—stick figures will do!).

Some of my workshop participants have told me that they don't dream. I tell them that generally, as long as we get more than a couple of hours of sleep at a time, we do tend to dream. But in order to remember our dreams, we often need to make a conscious effort to remember them. Once we begin to pay attention to our dreams, they will become clearer, more detailed and we are much more likely to remember them.

One of the best ways to remember your dreams is to record them, immediately upon awakening, in a journal that is kept by your bed. Starting your early morning routine, or switching into your busy-mind mode can make your dreams disappear into the Ether.

Food for Thought:

Do you remember your dreams?
Do you pay attention to your dreams?

Your Assignment:

Over the next week, begin your days by recording your dreams in the Dream Diary at the back of this workbook. Take just a few minutes each morning to write down the things you remember about your dreams, before you jumpstart your day. Write down your dreams in the present tense and make sure and note any feelings each dream evoked.

At the end of the week, read over your dreams. Ask yourself the following questions about each of your dreams:

1. Why were people in my dream doing what they were doing?

2. What part or parts of me was this dream showing?

3. What do the different objects and places in the dream represent to me?

4. Was the dream showing me something about myself that I don't usually think about?

5. Now, think of all of your dreams as a series—what themes did you see emerge over the course of week?

Recommended Reading

Dreams

Carl Gustav Jung, R. F. Hull, Translator (Princeton University Press, 1974)

Inner Work: Using Dreams & Active Imagination For Personal Growth

Robert Johnson (Harper, 1989)

5

What's Your Style?

"Man's main task in life is to give birth to himself, to become what he potentially is. The most important product of his effort is his own personality."

—*Erich Fromm*

"The meeting of two personalities is like the contact of two chemical substances: if there is any reaction, both are transformed."

—*Carl Jung*

How do you see the world? How do you approach tasks? How do you prefer to interact with other people? What types of activities do you enjoy?

You have probably heard of, or have even taken, one of the many personality tests that exist. Although they vary in terms of their scientific validity, personality tests can be useful tools for self-development, if you use reliable ones. As long as they are not used to label people, but rather to identify our natural preferences, and learn about our natural strengths and weaknesses within various environments, they can help us understand how we are likely to deal with different situations that life presents, and in which environments we are most likely to be comfortable. Knowing our preferences and style can help us to better understand ourselves.

Just as when we find ourselves in situations that are incompatible with our core values, when we find ourselves in situations or roles that are incompatible with our personal preferences, we tend to perform less than optimally and find ourselves unhappy. When we are in roles and environments that support our personal preferences, we tend to feel good about ourselves, we feel energized, and as a result we are more effective in all that we do.

One of the most well known, and widely used personality tests in the Myers-Briggs type indicator, which is based on the work of Carl Jung, Katharine Briggs and Isabel Briggs Myers.

Carl Jung developed the theory that individuals each have a psychological "type." He believed that there were three basic functions that we use to interact with the world: perceiving information, either via our senses or our intuition; and making decisions, either based on thinking and objective logic or subjective feelings. Jung believed that we all use these four functions in our lives, but that each individual uses each of the functions to differing degrees. By identifying the functions that individuals use most frequently (their "preference" for each function), we can define the individual's personality type.

Katharine C. Briggs further developed Jung's theory of personality types. Katharine's daughter, Isabel Briggs Myers, built upon her mother's work and Jung's work, and added another set of functions to Jung's original three based on the individual's day-to-day lifestyle preference—Judging versus Perceiving. This combined effort resulted in sixteen personality types based on the following:

1. Our flow of energy—the extent to which we prefer to receive stimulation from within ourselves (Introverted) versus external sources (Extraverted)

2. How we take in information—the extent to which we prefer to take in information via our five senses (Sensing) versus our instincts (Intuitive)

3. How we prefer to make decisions—the extent to which we make decisions based on logic and objective consideration (Thinking) versus our personal, subjective value systems (Feeling).

4. Our preferred basic day-to-day lifestyle—the extent to which we are organized and purposeful, and more comfortable with scheduled, structured environments (Judging) versus flexible and diverse, and more comfortable with open, casual environments (Perceiving)

As I've already mentioned, while we all use all of these modes to some extent, we all naturally have a preference within each category. According to the Myers-Briggs schema, the combination of our four "preferences" defines our personality type, for a total of 16 possible personality types under which you can fall, e.g. Extraverted Sensing Feeling Perceiving (ESFP), Introverted Sensing Thinking Judging (ISTJ), etc. This does not mean that all (or even most) individuals will fall strictly into one category or another. However, just because a person is primarily Extraverted, for example, does not mean that she doesn't also perform Introverted activities. We all function in all of these realms on a daily basis. Learning about our Personality Type helps us to understand why certain areas in life come easily to us, and others are more of a struggle. Learning about other people's Personality Types helps us to understand the most effective way to communicate with them, and how they function best.

In the early 1990s, psychologists Paul Costa, Jr. and Robert McCrae published a new theory of personality, which further expands upon the work of Jung, Myers and Briggs. The Big Five theory of personality traits differs from the Myers-Briggs theory of personality types, in that it goes beyond 16 categories in which people can fall, and rather looks at where each person falls on a continuum within the individual traits. In addition, it is based on five dimensions of personality (obviously), versus the four of the other theory. Thus, it allows for a greater range of ways in which to see people's personalities. The Big Five personality traits are as follows:

Extraversion: Sociability and outgoingness versus introversion; characterized by warmth, gregariousness, assertiveness, activity, excitement seeking and positive emotions.

Neuroticism: Emotional instability versus stability; characterized by anxiety, depression, hostility, self-consciousness, impulsiveness and vulnerability.

Openness to experience: Curiosity and interest in variety versus preference for sameness; characterized by openness to aesthetics, imagination, feelings, actions, ideas and values.

Agreeableness: Compliance and cooperativeness versus suspiciousness; characterized by trust, straightforwardness, altruism, compliance, modesty and tender-mindedness.

Conscientiousness: Discipline and organization versus lack of seriousness; characterized by competence, order, dutifulness, striving toward achievement, self-discipline and deliberation.

While the Big Five theory is a somewhat more realistic way of categorizing the ways in which personality manifests itself in our behaviors and attitudes than the Myers-Briggs, it is still a relatively new theory, so has yet to gain a foothold in the minds of the majority of people outside of academia.

Food for Thought:

How would you describe your personality?
How would your close friends and family describe you?
How would your acquaintances describe you?
How would your current or former colleagues describe you?

Your Assignment:

Over the course of the next few days, think about your style of interacting with the world and how it influences the way you relate to other people and approach the work that you do. And think about how others see you in the context of your home, family, work, etc.

If you are interested in finding out about your Personality Type, it is recommended that you take the Myers-Briggs Type Indicator® published by Consulting Psychologists Press, Inc., and look into the many books that give thorough descriptions of jobs that are compatible with various personality types.

Recommended Reading

Introduction to Type: A Guide to Understanding Your Results on the Myers-Briggs Type Indicator

> Isabel Briggs Myers (Center for Applications of Psychological Type, 1998)

The Big Five Personality Factors

> Boele DeRaad (Hogrefe & Huber, 2000)

The Big Five Assessment

> Boele DeRaad, Editor (Hogrefe & Huber, 2002)

Gifts Differing: Understanding Personality Type

> Isabela Myers Briggs (Consulting Psychologists Press, reprinted 1995)

Please Understand Me II: Temperament, Character, Intelligence

> David Keirsey (Prometheus Nemesis Book Company, 1998)

Do What You Are: Discover the Perfect Career for You Through the Secrets of Personality Type—Revised and Updated Edition Featuring E-careers for the 21st Century

> Paul D. Tieger and Barbara Barron-Tieger (Little Brown & Company, 2001)

Web Resources

Big Five Personality Test—this 48-item online questionnaire measures the five fundamental dimensions of personality

> http://www.outofservice.com/bigfive/

The Big Five Quickstart: An Introduction to the Five-Factor Model of Personality for Human Resource Professionals—from the Center for Applied Cognitive Studies

> http://www.centacs.com/quickstart.htm

The Kiersey Temperament Sorter II—based on the Myers-Briggs Type Inventory

> http://www.advisorteam.com

6

Take Inventory of Your Transferable Skills

"When love and skill work together, expect a masterpiece."

—*John Ruskin*

"Skill and confidence are an unconquered army."

—*George Herbert*

No matter what you choose to do next in your life, chances are that if you've been on this planet for a while, you've had a chance to develop several skills. As you plan to venture into a new career area, it is very helpful to take inventory of all your transferable skills—skills that you've acquired through experience, as well as your general abilities and aptitudes that can apply to any career that you may be interested in. Examples of transferable skills include planning, organizing, writing and analyzing. As you are thinking about what you might like to do next in your life, keep in mind that the skills needed in the new economy are flexibility, innovation, open communication, and openness to diversity.

In addition to transferable skills, we all have personal traits that can be important in a variety of careers. These include attitudes and characteristics such as empathy, patience, diplomacy, and independence. Think of the positive traits that you have developed throughout your lifetime, which may be important in various work settings. Research has found that personality traits such as creativity, leadership, integrity, attentiveness and cooperation play as important a role in job success as do skills and abilities. And, of all personality traits, the Big Five trait of Conscientiousness (characterized as being responsible, dependable, organized and persistent) has been found to consistently predict performance in all levels and types of jobs, except for very creative ones: interestingly, it seems the best musicians and artists are not always the most conscientious individuals.

You will also have acquired knowledge-based skills along the way. These include technical knowledge, procedures or job-specific information necessary to perform a task, function or job. Knowledge-based skills can be acquired through paid and non-paid experiences, education, training and hobbies. They can include skills such as web design, bookkeeping, home remodeling, early childhood development and party planning.

Employers are interested in knowing which skills you can bring to their organization. A functional resume, which focuses on specific skills rather than the chronology of the work that you've done, is a great way to highlight them. Think about your past experiences, including jobs, volunteer work, academic and personal activities as you begin to create a thorough inventory of your skills, traits and abilities. Make sure that you include such seemingly basic skills as oral and written communication, time management, research and problem solving, as they are considered among the top ten most desirable skills in the eyes of employers. At the end of this chapter, I have listed a couple of websites that provide examples of functional resumes, which are arranged by groups of skills, rather than in chronological job order.

Volunteer experiences definitely count. Deborah had been a full-time mother for 24 years. As she began to seriously consider working in the field of human resources, she worried that she would have few of the necessary skills. However, in reflecting upon her many years of volunteer work and the skills it takes to run a household, she realized that she had acquired many critical skills that could apply to any job, and several that would apply directly to a career working to help people.

And it appears that it does not matter in what context you acquire such skills, but just having the skills will best predict your success in a given career. A recent study by psychologists Phillip Ackerman and Anna Cianciolo revealed that people do best in jobs for which they have specific skills and abilities. First, they tested individuals for various skills, including language, numeric and spatial. They then tested the same individuals' performance in a variety of tasks of increasing complexity, which utilized these basic skills. They found that basic skills were good predictors of individual performance regardless of context. For example, numerical ability predicted success in bookkeeping as well as accounting.

If you are interested in having a formal assessment of your basic skills and aptitudes, I recommend that you find a psychologist or other qualified tester who can administer the Differential Aptitude Test for Personnel and Career Assessment (DAT), which is published by the Psychological Corporation. The DAT is an assessment of how well you are likely to do in different work and study areas. It is made up of the following subtests: Verbal Reasoning; Numerical Ability; Abstract Reasoning; Mechanical Reasoning; Spatial Relations; Language Usage; Clerical; and Spelling.

Food for Thought:

Which achievements make you proudest? Which ones did you find the most challenging? Which ones gave you the biggest thrill?

Your Assignment:

Think about your past experiences, and take note of the ones that hold meaning for you, the achievements that make you proud. Begin by listing eight achievements you have experienced during the past few years in the Achievement Inventory at the back of this book. They can be anything that you've done that has been meaningful to you, and can include experiences in the following areas, or anything else you can think of:

- Work experience
- Volunteer experiences
- Awards/honors
- Activities
- Hobbies
- Relationships
- Classes
- Team/group involvement
- New skills
- Travel
- Special projects

As you describe each achievement, list the skills, abilities, or personal traits that were most important in making each of the experiences meaningful and productive for you. Once you have completed this exercise, look for patterns across your experiences in terms of skills, settings, or types of people that were involved.

Web Resources

Examples of functional resumes

http://www1.umn.edu/ohr/ecep/resume/function.htm

http://leo.stcloudstate.edu/resumes/functresum1.html

7

You Gotta Have Friends

"When I find myself fading, I close my eyes and realize my friends are my energy."

—*Anonymous*

"Friendship makes prosperity more shining and lessens adversity by dividing and sharing it."

—*Cicero*

"A friendship can weather most things and thrive in thin soil; but it needs a little mulch of letters and phone calls and small, silly presents every so often—just to save it from drying out completely."

—*Pam Brown*

As humans, we need other people—it's a basic part of our nature. Social support is the academic term for the love, respect, acknowledgement, help, encouragement, friendship, kinship, backing, etc. that you get from friends, family and professionals (e.g. doctors, clergy, lawyers, therapists, etc.) in your life. And while we each vary in terms of the extent of our need for social support, the fact remains that people need people.

Research by psychologists and epidemiologists such as James House, Walter Broadhead, Cathy Sherbourne, and Barbara and Irwin Sarason has shown that support from others strongly influences our mental as well as physical health. Positive social support has been found to enhance our self-esteem, our sense of physical and mental well-being, reduces the incidence of stress and depression, boosts our immune systems, lowers our risk of all sorts of illnesses, enhances and supports treatment and recovery from illness and addiction, and can even slow biological aging!

Early in 2003, psychologist Laura Cousin Klein published a study that indicates that social support is especially important for women in helping to reduce the effects of stress. It seems that the hormone oxytocin is released in response to stress and, for women, "tending and befriending," or nurturing one's social ties, actually helps to release additional oxytocin, further reducing stress and producing a calming effect. Prior to this discovery, 90% of stress research had been conducted on men, for whom the natural response to stress tends to be "fight or flight."

Within the workplace, social support from family, friends and colleagues continues to be very important. Psychologists Jeffrey Greenhaus and Stewart Friedman found that people who extend their social networks on the job are more satisfied with family life, and have healthier more academically successful children than those who tend to keep to themselves. Psychologists Joseph Grzywacz and Nadine Marks also found that people with more social support at work are less likely to report work-family conflicts than people with less work-based social support. As mentioned earlier, the combination of work *and* family can be beneficial for men and women: Grzywacz and Marks also found that participants with families reported that having someone to talk to at home about work problems helped them to deal with work-related stressors, and made them feel more confident about themselves at work. Similarly, psychologists Leslie Hammer and Margaret Neal found that having a good support network at work reduces work-family conflict and actually has a positive affect on spouse's job satisfaction. Another win-win situation!

While support from friends and family is generally a good thing, it can, at times, be more of a burden than a blessing. Sometimes support comes in the form of over-involvement, overprotection, well-intended-but-misguided advice, enabling of unhealthy behaviors, or help given with strings attached. Remember the stories in Chapter 2—if these people had listened to their well-intentioned family members, they would not be involved in the fulfilling work they are doing now.

In my research, I have found that support is very important, in general friends for women and family for men. Again, good, positive support has been shown to lead to better outcomes. And it's about quality not quantity—even one very good friend or family member can make all the difference.

So it is well-established that it is important, for many reasons, to build and maintain your social and business networks. As you explore new career options, you can benefit from joining business networking groups, joining associations related to the fields you are interested in, attending conferences or volunteering in the areas you are exploring. You can also leverage your existing social networks—do you have friends, family or acquaintances who might know about the fields you are interested in? Perhaps they know someone else who does. As long as you have a good rapport with them, most people will be more than happy to share their knowledge, advice and leads with you.

Food for Thought:

Who are the important people in your life? Do they support you? Is their support helpful?

Your Assignment:

1. Write down the names of the people who are an important part of your life. Who are they? What are their roles?

2. As you move forward with your career plans, choose one or two people that you would like to tell your plans to. In this way, you will create support for your goals, since you will make yourself "accountable" to them. Ask them to check in with you from week to week regarding your progress, challenges, victories, stumbling blocks, etc. It helps to get feedback, and it is motivating to know that someone is there watching your journey and supporting your efforts.

   Name of Support Person: _____

   Name of Support Person: _____

3. Nurture your existing network. Schedule coffee, breakfast, lunch, dinner, or any amount of time you can spare with one friend per week over the next 8 weeks. It's a great way to catch up with your friends and acquaintances, and it will give you a chance to talk to people about what you are working on.

4. Take steps to expand your social networks. Look into local business networking opportunities and membership in professional organizations related to your fields of interest. There are also online networking communities that offer free memberships and access to many special interest groups, as well as real-life monthly meetings organized by members.

Ryze and Company of Friends are two excellent examples that you may want to look into. I've listed their website addresses below.

Web Resources

Company of Friends—grassroots network of readers of Fast Company Magazine

http://www.fastcompany.com/cof

Ryze—an online business networking resource

http://www.ryze.com

Social Support Survey Form—from Cathy Sherbourne's work on *The Medical Outcomes Study*

http://www.rand.org/health/surveys/mos.survey.html

8

So What's Next?

"Success is not the result of spontaneous combustion. You must set yourself on fire."

—*Reggie Leach*

"If your success is not on your own terms, if it looks good to the world but does not feel good in your heart, it is not success at all."

—*Anna Quindlen*

Congratulations! In the last 7 weeks or so, you have done a lot of introspection; have taken inventory of your values, interests and resources. You have worked to better understand your needs and wants in a career. Now it's time to bring it all together and create an action plan for yourself.

So, are you ready to start working on the career path that you've chosen? As you've seen, there is ample research showing that you can be happy and achieve your goals if you have confidence in yourself, focus on your path, foster relationships with others and keep your mind open to possibilities.

Continue to work toward weekly goals, adding new steps or modifying existing ones as you move forward. Continue to utilize the exercises in *It's Your Time Now*, as needed. And, most importantly, enjoy your journey into the next chapter of your life!

Food for Thought:

What are your overall goals for moving toward your ideal career?

Your Assignment:

1. Answer the following questions as thoroughly as you can:

    a. What ONE step can you take tomorrow to move closer to your ideal career?

    b. What steps can you take in next month to move closer to your ideal career?

    c. What obstacles might keep you from achieving your goals?

    d. How can you overcome those obstacles? (Example: strong motivation, support of friends and family, educational resources)

    e. What resources do you have to support your goals? (Example: marketable/transferable skills, support network of friends, family or professionals, sources of income)

2. Thinking about the characteristics of your ideal job, make a list of the jobs that are potentially interesting to you. You may want to consider a source like the Occupational Outlook Handbook (available at your local library) for ideas.

3. Fill out the following contract with yourself and give a copy to your support persons

I, _____, promise myself to do the following:

Within the next week, I will do the following to work toward my career goals:

Within the next month, I will do the following to work toward my career goals

I will join the following networks

I will look into the following job or volunteer opportunities

I will seek support from the following people, and will hold myself accountable by checking in with them on a regular basis regarding my progress

Recommended Reading

Occupational Outlook Handbook 2002–2003

   United States Department of Labor (VGM Career Books, 2002)

Web Resources

The Art & The Science—Mary Guarino's life coaching website

   http://www.theartandthescience.com

Values Log

Dream Diary

Good Stuff Log

Ideal Work Environment Log

Achievement Inventory

Achievement 1:

Achievement 2:

Achievement 3:

Achievement 4:

Achievement 5:

Achievement 6:

Achievement 7:

Achievement 8:

About the Author

Mary Guarino is a life coach specializing in helping people who are in career and life transitions make the next phase of their lives fulfilling, joyous and meaningful. She holds a B.A. in Fine Arts, a Ph.D. in Lifespan Developmental Psychology, and completed her coaching training through the Institute for Life Coaching. In addition to individual coaching, Mary offers workshops in New York City and Fairfield County, CT. Her workshop series *It's Your Time Now: What Will You Do With It?* was the inspiration for this book.

In her work as a psychologist, Mary's research focused on social support and health care usage. She also has 7 years of corporate experience in the area of consumer attitudinal research. Prior to her work in psychology, research and life coaching, Mary was an artist and graphic designer. She continues to create her artwork. Mary lives in Weston, Connecticut with her two wonderful adolescent daughters.

For information on her coaching practice and upcoming workshops, or if you have any questions regarding the completion of this workbook, please feel free to email her at maryg@theartandthescience.com.

0-595-30320-X

Made in the USA
Lexington, KY
15 June 2011